Southern MODIFIED

"SOUTHERN INSPIRED DISHES, MODIFIED FOR TODAY'S HEALTHIER LIFESTYLE"

CHEF JERNARD WELLS
AND ACTRESS
DENISE BOUTTÉ

authorHOUSE®

AuthorHouse™
1663 Liberty Drive
Bloomington, IN 47403
www.authorhouse.com
Phone: 1 (800) 839-8640

Published by AuthorHouse 04/12/2018

ISBN: 978-1-5462-3125-7 (sc)
ISBN: 978-1-5462-3123-3 (hc)
ISBN: 978-1-5462-3124-0 (e)

Library of Congress Control Number: 2018902559

Print information available on the last page.

Any people depicted in stock imagery provided by Getty Images are models, and such images are being used for illustrative purposes only. Certain stock imagery © Getty Images.

This book is printed on acid-free paper.

Because of the dynamic nature of the Internet, any web addresses or links contained in this book may have changed since publication and may no longer be valid. The views expressed in this work are solely those of the author and do not necessarily reflect the views of the publisher, and the publisher hereby disclaims any responsibility for them.

Table of Contents

Nard and Neesie's Ultimate Veggie Burger

Denise's *Modified* Faves

SOUTHERN SIGNATURES

SLOW COOKER FAVES

SUPER SALADS

FEATURED EXTRAS... SNACKS!

SHOW-STOPPING MAIN COURSES

SCENE-STEALING VEGGIES

VIP SMOOTHIES

Chef Jernard's Vegan Lifestyle

VEGETARIAN DELIGHT

WEEKEND DELIGHTS

STRESS-FREE COOKING

SUNDAY DELIGHTS

MISSISSIPPI COMFORT

CHEF OF LOVE SWEET TREATS

Mississippi joins forces with Louisiana!

When Chef Wells and I were brainstorming the perfect dish to join forces on, low and behold it was the infamous veggie burger that appeared on both our lists. While I appreciate the attempts of chefs past, this trendy menu item had yet to please my palate… That is, until Chef Jernard and I developed the Ultimate *Modified* Veggie Burger. You may have tried veggie burgers in the past, but this beauty goes Far beyond just being healthy. The elusive pursuit of the perfect veggie burger, Stops Here!

Nard and Neesie's Ultimate Veggie Burger

Ingredients

Burger

1 (15-ounce) can chickpeas
1/2 cup chopped red onion
1 tablespoon minced garlic
10 minced baby bella mushrooms
2 tablespoons finely chopped cilantro
2 tablespoons barbecue sauce
1 teaspoon Thai chili sauce
2 tablespoons roasted red-pepper hummus
1 packet gumbo seasoning
1 teaspoon garlic powder
1 teaspoon ground black pepper
1/2 teaspoon sea salt
1 cup seasoned breadcrumbs
1 tablespoon extra-virgin olive oil
pretzel buns or baked portobello mushroom caps

Optional Toppings

Grilled onions
Avocado, sliced
Lime wedge
Bibb lettuce
Tomato
Pickles
Condiments

Directions

- Drain and then rinse chickpeas. Pour into bowl and mash with fork. Set aside.
- In food processor, combine onion, garlic, mushrooms, cilantro, barbecue sauce, chili sauce, hummus, gumbo seasoning, garlic powder, black pepper, sea salt, bread crumbs and olive oil. Pulse until smooth.
- Add mixture to bowl with chickpeas. Mix and combine thoroughly with hands.
- Form ball then pat to flatten into patty about 3/4-inch thick. Will yield 6–8 patties.
- Heat skillet or grill to 350 degrees F. Cook patties for 10 minutes on each side.
- As patties cook, grill split, pretzel buns, cut-side down for a total of 3 minutes; For mushroom buns, clean inside of Portobello mushroom caps, rub with oil on both sides, and grill until they are soft and tender.
- Once buns are removed from skillet or grill, add preferred toppings to burger and savor the flavor of this *Modified* Masterpiece!

DENISE BOUTTÉ

My name is Denise Boutté and I have a confession... I LOVE FOOD! Cooking is simply part of who I am. Where I come from... We Celebrate? We eat! We mourn? We eat. It's simply part of my DNA! I grew up just a bike ride away from my Mon Mon and Papa's farm. It was bustling with livestock and thriving with acres of soybeans, sweet potatoes, okra, sugarcane, you name it! Guess you can call me the real life Queen Sugar!

It wasn't until I moved next door to Texas, that I learned to truly value and appreciate the simplicity, with which I was raised. Even in the midst of what some call Holly-Weird, the core of my being remains the same.... Faith, Family, Food and Fun!

Upon moving to California, cooking began to manifest from pastime into passion. It became a resource— Not only a way to reconnect and realign with pre-mom Denise, but also an additional outlet for expressing my creativity, beyond the set. While a Chef develops a keen knowledge of food science, I compensated with natural ability and heightened sensibilities of sight, smell, texture and taste, to skillfully modify traditional family favorites. I made a conscious decision, to be mindful of what my family and I put into our body, mind and spirit machines.

Developed according to my "everything in moderation" school of thought, *Southern Modified* features healthy and palate-pleasing versions of everything from Gumbo to Kale Chips. So go ahead... Use that imagination, be open to exploring new territory and dig in! I promise you'll discover modified dishes and tips that you and your family will add to the favorites list and enjoy for many years to come!

XoXo- DB'

For all things Denise Boutté, follow me online!

Facebook: Denise Boutte
Instagram: @Denise_Boutte
Twitter: @Denise_Boutte
www.WeezianaGirl.com

JERNARD WELLS

As the 2016 (Season 12) runner-up on *Food Network Star*, celebrity TV chef and best-selling author Jernard Wells has acquired fans from all over the world. He has appeared as a judge on the Food Network hit show *Chopped Junior*, is a two-time winner on *Cutthroat Kitchen*, and has been in the top ten of the World Food Championships for three years in a row. Already a best-selling author, Chef Jernard has written such titles as *88 Ways To Her Heart—Cooking for Lovers*, *Weight of Expectations, Breakthrough,* and *Road Map: A Woman's Guide to a Good Man.* He has made many appearances around the US, including the 2017 Essence Festival in New Orleans, is a regular contributor to the Food Network, and participated in the New York City Wine and Food Festival.

A successful entrepreneur, Chef Jernard has his own manufacturing company; his amazing line of sauces and seasonings, Le' Chef Amours Haute Cuisine, can be purchased in retail stores across the globe and also at www.chefjernard.com. In addition, he has a branded line of cutlery and cookware by Gunter Williams Knives and Cookware, called Uncivilized by Chef Jernard.

Chef Jernard cofounded Compete Wells—the official World Food Championships competitor series. Compete Wells is an official qualifying event, where chefs, foodies, and pit masters from around the country are trained by Chef Wells and then go on to compete for a "golden ticket," which allows them to participate in the World Food Championships—the largest food sport in the world—for a chance at winning $100,000.

For all things Chef Jernard Wells, follow me online!

Facebook: Jernard Wells

Instagram: @chefjernard

Twitter: @chefjernard

www.chefjernard.com

SOUTHERN SIGNATURES

Holy Trinity of Louisiana Cooking… Plus Garlic!

Nothing says "nostalgia" quite like these Louisiana staples. My desire to use healthier ingredients was carefully balanced by the vital responsibility of maintaining traditional flavor profiles. While the texture and overall integrity of each dish retains the cozy comfort you remember, I've tweaked to support the healthier lifestyles that we and our families need, deserve, and desire. Presenting Signature, down-home favorites… *Modified!*

Weeziana Girl Gumbo

Ingredients

Dark Roux
1 cup extra-virgin olive oil (okra oil is an alternative)
1 cup all-purpose flour (brown rice flour is an alternative)

Gumbo
2 quarts chicken stock
2 pounds medium shrimp
3 tablespoons extra-virgin olive oil, divided
3 tablespoons Weeziana Girl Low Sodium Seasoning, divided
3 tablespoons garlic powder, divided
2 cups water
2 smoked turkey drumsticks
1 can smoked oysters
1/4 cup dried shrimp, ground into powder
2 cups chopped yellow onion
1/2 cup chopped celery
1 cup green bell pepper, cored, seeded and chopped
1/2 cup red bell pepper, cored, seeded and chopped
3 tablespoons minced garlic
5 boneless, skinless chicken thighs (or 4 breast halves)
2 pounds smoked chicken sausage, halved, then sliced 1/4-inch thick
1 (8-ounce) package turkey tasso, diced
1/4 cup fresh chopped parsley leaves
2 cups sliced green onions
2 pounds crab legs (blue, snow, etc.)
Cooked rice for serving (optional)
Water to adjust thickness (optional)

Directions

- For roux, in a heavy-bottomed Dutch oven, combine equal parts oil and flour. Cook over medium-high heat, stirring constantly until it turns the color of milk chocolate, approximately 30 minutes. Do not burn!
- Add chicken stock while whisking briskly. Simmer over medium-low heat. As necessary, add water to achieve desired consistency.
- Peel and devein shrimp, but save the shells and set aside. In a separate bowl, mix together shrimp, olive oil, Weeziana Girl seasoning and garlic powder. Cover and place in refrigerator.
- Place shells in small saucepan and fill with water until covered. Once boiling, turn down to a low simmer. Cook 15–20 minutes and then strain the stock into the Dutch oven.
- Now for the coup de grâce, a.k.a., the secret weapon—Smoked Turkey Legs! Add the smoked turkey legs to the Dutch oven. (Special thanks to T-Peg for upping my gumbo game by showing me the beauty that is smoked turkey and smoked oysters. Delish!)
- Add smoked oysters and dried shrimp to Dutch oven and increase heat to medium.
- Add onions, celery, bell peppers, fresh garlic and garlic powder.
- While flavor tango commences in the Dutch oven, chop chicken into bite-size chunks and season with remaining Weeziana Girl, garlic powder and 1 tablespoon olive oil.
- Heat remaining tablespoon oil in large skillet over medium-high heat. Add seasoned chicken and sausage, stirring often until well browned, about 10 minutes. Once removed from pot, set aside to cool while proceeding to sauté shrimp for 7 minutes. Set aside.
- The longer you cook, the better! Reduce heat to medium-low and allow to simmer, uncovered, for 2 hours.
- Once 1 hour of cook time remains, add diced tasso, browned chicken, sausage, parsley and green onions (or as we Louisiana folk call them, onion tops).
- Prepare rice according to directions.
- By now, smoked turkey legs are "fall-off-bone" ready. Remove from pot with slotted spoon. Detach delectable chunks of meat from the

skin, center bone and smaller bone shards. Reintroduce meat chunks to the Dutch oven. Discard scraps.

- When half-hour of cook time remains, add crab legs and sautéed shrimp.
- Remove from heat and rest for 15 minutes
- Enjoy as is or spoon over cooked rice.

Gumbos are just as varied as our individual taste buds,
so have fun! Get creative with your ingredients.
—D. Boutté

Weeziana Girl Rotisserie Chicken Pot Pie

Ingredients

Gluten-Free Pie Crust

Although I'm skilled at making from scratch, my pot pie crust usually isn't homemade. My reasoning? Sometimes cutting corners just makes sense, especially when school's in session. With so many frozen options available in the health-food store, I vote for saving precious time and focusing on the filling.

Filling

2 cups chicken stock

2 carrots, peeled and sliced into 1/4-inch rounds

1 large baking potato, scrubbed, peeled, and cut into 1/2-inch cubes

3 tablespoons extra-virgin olive oil

1 cup chopped yellow onion

1/2 cup green bell pepper, cored, seeded and chopped

1 rib celery, finely chopped

2 tablespoons minced garlic

1 teaspoon fresh minced thyme

1/4 teaspoon ground black pepper

1 teaspoon garlic powder

2 tablespoons all-purpose flour

1 (14.75-ounce) can creamed sweet corn

1 rotisserie chicken, deboned

1/2 cup sliced green onions

1 cup frozen French-cut green beans

1 cup frozen sweet peas, thawed

1/4 cup fresh chopped parsley leaves

Extra-virgin olive oil cooking spray

1 teaspoon Weeziana Girl Low Sodium Seasoning

1 1/2 cups frozen extra sweet whole kernel corn

Directions

- Preheat oven to 400 degrees F.
- In a small saucepan over high heat, bring chicken stock and sea salt to a boil. Add carrots and potatoes. Boil until just tender, about 10 minutes.
- With slotted spoon, remove carrots and potatoes from pot and set aside. Reserve stock.
- In a large skillet, heat olive oil over medium-high heat.
- Add onions, bell pepper, celery, fresh garlic, thyme, black pepper and garlic powder.
- Stir often and cook until vegetables are softened but not charred, about 5 minutes. If at any time mixture begins to stick to pan, use some reserved chicken stock to deglaze.
- It's now time to thicken! Stir in flour and creamed corn. Reduce heat to medium low and simmer.
- Rotisserie chicken time! Pull meat from bones, chop into bite-size chunks.
- Add to skillet, the chicken, green onions, green beans, thawed peas and parsley. Allow to simmer for an additional 15 minutes.
- As simmer continues, lightly coat casserole dish with cooking spray. On flat surface, roll out 2 piecrusts. Place first in dish and gently press to line bottom and side surfaces, leaving a bit of overlap. This will be used to adhere to surface crust.
- Back to skillet. Add Weeziana Girl to taste and fold in whole kernel corn. Use any remaining stock to achieve desired consistency
- Pour filling into lined casserole dish and spread evenly
- Cover dish with second piecrust, making sure to seal by pinching top crust, to overlap of bottom. Cut 5 or so, small slits into top crust.
- Bake for 30 minutes, or until crust is golden brown.
- Remove from oven. Allow to rest for 15 minutes. Serve!

*Smoked turkey, smoked oysters and dried shrimp. This
trifecta will ensure you "put yo foot up in that pot!"*
                                                    —*D. Boutté*

Weeziana Girl Shrimp Creole

Ingredients

Light Roux
1/4 cup extra-virgin olive oil
1/4 cup all-purpose flour (brown rice flour is an alternative)

Creole Sauce
2 pounds medium shrimp
1 tablespoon extra-virgin olive oil
3 tablespoons Weeziana Girl Low Sodium Seasoning
1 teaspoon garlic powder
3 cups chicken stock
1 tablespoon vegan butter
1 cup minced yellow onion
1/2 bundle sliced green onions
1/2 cup green bell pepper, cored, seeded and finely chopped
1 rib celery, finely chopped
2 tablespoons minced garlic
1 (14.5-ounce) can diced basil, garlic, oregano tomatoes
1 (6-ounce) can tomato paste
1 (10.75-ounce) can condensed tomato soup
1/4 cup fresh chopped cilantro
1 teaspoon fresh chopped oregano, packed
1 1/2 teaspoons fresh chopped basil, packed
1/2 teaspoon fresh chopped thyme, packed
1/4 cup fresh parsley leaves, chopped
1/2 teaspoon ground black pepper
1/4 teaspoon chipotle chili pepper, chopped
3/4 teaspoon organic brown sugar
Cooked rice for serving (optional)

Directions

- Peel and devein shrimp. Mix shrimp with olive oil, 1 tablespoon Weeziana Girl and garlic powder. Cover and place in refrigerator.
- This dish requires a light roux, as opposed to dark version used in gumbo recipe. While cooking technique is the same, cook time is the variable. In a heavy-bottom Dutch oven, combine equal parts olive olive oil and flour. Cook over medium-high heat, stirring constantly until it turns the color of peanut butter, approximately 15 minutes. Thanks to Momma Betty, I always keep a jar nearby, for perfect color reference ;-)
- Slowly whisk in 1/3 cup of chicken stock and vegan butter, then add yellow onions, green onions, bell pepper, celery and garlic. Sautee for 10 minutes.
- Add remaining stock, diced tomato, tomato paste and tomato soup.
- Once combined, bring on the fresh herbs: cilantro, oregano, basil, thyme and parsley.
- To this mixture add black pepper, chipotle pepper, remaining 2 tablespoons of Weeziana Girl and brown sugar. While I tend to use it sparingly in most dishes, cilantro indeed matters and takes this dish to the *next level*!
- Reduce heat to medium-low, allowing flavor tango to commence. Simmer uncovered for 1 hour.
- Prepare rice according to directions.
- When 15 minutes of cook time remains, lock in flavor by charring shrimp with a 5–7 minute sauté. Add to sauce and allow to cook for 3 additional minutes.
- Remove from heat and rest for 15 minutes.
- Enjoy as is or spoon over cooked rice.

My mom served countless Head Start kids, including yours truly, for over forty-five years. After cookin' up healthy meals on the job, she'd return home to do it all over again for the family. Love the woman you are, and the one you've helped me become.
                                                                    —*D. Boutté*

Nanny Reesa's Smothered Okra

Ingredients

3 pounds fresh okra, or 1(48-ounce) bag, if frozen

3 boneless, skinless chicken thighs (or 2 breast halves) cut into bite-size chunks

3 tablespoons Weeziana Girl Low Sodium Seasoning

3 tablespoons garlic powder

1/4 teaspoon ground black pepper

4 tablespoons extra-virgin olive oil

2 cups chicken broth

1 pound smoked chicken sausage, sliced into 1/4-inch-thick rounds

2 pounds medium shrimp

1 dozen blue crab claws (optional)

2 cups chopped yellow onions

1 cup green bell pepper, cored, seeded and chopped

2 tablespoons minced garlic

1/4 cup distilled white vinegar

2 tablespoons dried shrimp, ground into powder

1 (8-ounce) can tomato sauce

2 (10-ounce) cans of chopped Rotel tomatoes

2 tablespoons agave nectar

Cooked rice for serving (optional)

Directions

- If purchased fresh, wash okra under warm water. Trim off stems and tips, then chop into 1/4-inch slices (the thicker you slice, the longer it'll take to cook). Set aside.
- Roughly chop chicken thighs, season with 1 tablespoon Weeziana Girl, 1 tablespoon garlic powder, black pepper and 1 tablespoon olive oil. Cover and refrigerate.
- In Dutch oven, heat 1 tablespoon olive oil and sauté chicken sausage over medium-high heat for 3 minutes, stirring often. Remove from pot and set aside.
- Tip: If sticking occurs at any point during cooking, use broth to deglaze (1 tablespoon at a time).
- Add seasoned chicken thighs, stirring often until well browned, about 10 minutes. Remove from pot, cover and set aside.
- Peel and devein shrimp. Mix with 1 tablespoon olive oil, 1 tablespoon Weeziana Girl and 1 tablespoon garlic powder. Sauté for 5–10 minutes, stirring frequently. Set aside.
- Heat final tablespoon of olive oil over medium-high heat, add okra, onions, bell pepper, garlic, remaining broth, vinegar, dried shrimp, tomato sauce, chopped tomatoes, 1 tablespoon Weeziana Girl, 1 tablespoon garlic powder and agave nectar.
- Reduce heat to medium-low and simmer for 1 hour. Make sure to stir often, scraping bottom to prevent sticking.
- Prepare rice according to directions.
- When 1 hour of cook time remains, add sautéed chicken thighs.
- When 15 minutes of cook time remains, add sautéed chicken sausage, shrimp and optional crab claws.
- Enjoy as is or spoon over cooked rice.

Momma Betty's Cabbage Rolls

Ingredients

Cabbage
1 large head green cabbage
Water for boiling (enough to fill 1/3 of large pot)

Sauce
1 tablespoon extra-virgin olive oil
1/2 cup chopped yellow onion
2 teaspoons minced garlic
1 (14.5-ounce) can diced fire-roasted tomatoes
1 (10.75-ounce) can condensed tomato soup
1 packet (2 grams) stevia
1 tablespoon Weeziana Girl Low Sodium Seasoning

Stuffing
1 tablespoon extra-virgin olive oil
1 tablespoon minced garlic
1 cup chopped yellow onion
1/3 cup green bell pepper, cored, seeded and chopped
1/2 pound lean (80-percent) ground beef
1 pound ground turkey
3 tablespoons fresh chopped parsley
1 1/2 tablespoons Weeziana Girl Low Sodium Seasoning
1/2 teaspoon ground black pepper
1 cup prepared rice (slightly underdone)
1 large organic egg, beaten

Directions

- Preheat oven to 350 degrees F.
- In Dutch oven, bring water to a boil.
- With a sharp knife, carefully remove core of cabbage and discard, along with any damaged outer leaves. Carefully separate until you have a minimum of 15 whole leaves. (Don't waste good cabbage! Reserve any leftovers for "Sesame Mardi Gras Slaw" – see Super Salads section.)
- Blanch leaves until soft, 2–5 minutes. Set aside, allowing to cool. Discard water. Keep pot handy.
- In another pot, prepare rice according to directions, reducing cook time by 5 minutes so it's slightly underdone.
- In large skillet, heat olive oil over medium-high heat, adding onion and garlic for quick (7–10 minute) sauté.
- Add diced tomatoes, soup, stevia and Weeziana Girl. Reduce heat to medium-low and simmer for 15 minutes, allowing sauce to thicken. Remove from heat then spread 1/3 cup into 9-inch x 13-inch casserole dish.
- In previously used Dutch oven, heat olive oil then cook beef and turkey thoroughly, making sure to drain any fat before adding garlic, onion, bell pepper, parsley, Weeziana Girl, black pepper and cooked rice. Simmer for 5 minutes. Once cool, stir in egg.
- Get your roll on! Lay cabbage leaf, curved side up, onto flat surface and scoop 1/3 cup filling onto center. Starting from stem end, roll till filling enclosed, and then fold in sides to complete roll. Place seam-side down into dish, side by side. Repeat until complete.
- Pour remaining tomato sauce mixture over rolls, cover with foil and bake for 75–90 minutes.
- Remove from oven. Allow to rest for 15 minutes before serving.
- Yields approximately 1 dozen rolls.

SLOW COOKER FAVES

Mom and I at "Why Did I Get Married?" premiere.

Time to do the slow-cooker flavor tango! Before heading out of town for filming, I prepare a variety of favorites in batches, vacuum seal, label and freeze. Knowing the Fam has healthy go-to's, just a heat-and-eat away, comforts my spirit. The slow cooker is one of the most underappreciated appliances in the kitchen. Dust off that bad boy and create delectable meals, infusing layers of flavor with minimal effort. Depending on the dish, I usually simmer slow cooker recipes between 5 and 8 hours (in a 7-quart cooker). The longer the better!

Rotisserie Tortilla Soup with Chipotle

Ingredients:

Soup

2 tablespoons extra-virgin olive oil
1 1/2 cups chopped red onion
3/4 cup green bell pepper, cored, seeded and chopped
1 tablespoon garlic powder
1/4 teaspoon ground black pepper
1 1/2 tablespoons Weeziana Girl Low Sodium Seasoning
1 quart organic chicken stock
1 can 98-percent fat-free cream of chicken soup
1 tablespoon Worcestershire sauce
1 1/2 tablespoons crushed chipotle pepper
2 tablespoons chopped garlic
1/4 cup fresh chopped cilantro
1 teaspoon fresh minced thyme
1 (28-ounce) can black beans
1 (28-ounce) can diced tomatoes
1 smoked turkey drumstick
1 1/2 cups frozen extra-sweet whole-kernel corn
1 lime
1 rotisserie chicken, deboned
1 cup green onions

Optional Toppings

Smoked mozzarella, provolone, or Monterey jack cheese, grated
Avocado, sliced
Lime wedge
Tortilla strips
Crème fraîche or cream cheese

Directions:

- In a large skillet, heat olive oil over medium-high heat.
- Add onions, bell pepper, garlic powder, black pepper and 1/2 tablespoon Weeziana Girl.
- Stir often and cook until vegetables are softened but not charred, approximately 7 minutes.
- Add 1/4 cup chicken broth to mixture. Deglaze pot and pour into slow cooker.
- Whisk in cream of chicken soup, Worcestershire and chipotle.
- Add garlic, cilantro and minced thyme.
- Fold in black beans, diced tomatoes and remaining broth.
- Drop in smoked turkey drumstick. Cover.
- Remove chicken meat from bones and cut into bight-size chunks. Halfway through cook time, add chicken and green onions.
- Stirring occasionally, total cook time is 6-8 hours on low heat.
- Remove smoked turkey leg from pot with slotted spoon. Detach tender meat from skin, center bone and smaller bone shards. Reintroduce meat chunks to Dutch oven.
- Add remaining Weeziana Girl.
- When 15 minutes of cook time remain, add corn.
- If using avocado, squeeze on lime juice to prevent browning and shake on desired amount of Weeziana Girl.
- Once cook time is complete, ladle into bowl and enjoy as is or with toppings.

Split Pea Soup, Slow-Cooker Style

Ingredients:

1 pound split green peas, rinsed
1 pound bag frozen peas with
    onions, thawed
1 leek, finely chopped
1 rib celery, finely chopped
2 cups chopped yellow onion
1/2 cup red bell pepper, cored,
    seeded and chopped
1/2 cup fresh chopped parsley leaves

1 teaspoon chopped fresh thyme
3 carrots, peeled and chopped
1 quart (plus) chicken stock
2 tablespoons Weeziana Girl Low
    Sodium Seasoning
2 tablespoons garlic powder
1/4 teaspoon ground black pepper
2 smoked turkey drumsticks
1 cup sliced green onions

Optional Toppings
"Sesame Seared Shrimp" (see "Show-Stopping Main Courses")
Crème fraîche
Ground black pepper
Garlic croutons

Directions:

- Add split peas, frozen peas, leek, celery, onions, bell pepper, parsley, thyme, carrots and chicken stock to slow cooker.
- Stir in Weeziana Girl, garlic powder and black pepper. Drop in smoked turkey drumsticks. Cover.
- Stir occasionally. Total cook time is 6–8 hours on low heat.
- When 2 hours of cook time remain, use potato masher to smooth out some but not all peas. Remove smoked turkey from pot with slotted spoon. Detach now-tender meat from skin, center bone and smaller bone shards. Reintroduce meat chunks to slow cooker.
- Add green onions and if necessary, additional stock to achieve desired thickness.
- Once cook time is complete, ladle into bowl and enjoy as is or with toppings.

Before your Weeziana Girl goes into lights-camera-action mode, I up the ante on workouts and couple with hearty soups. This has me camera-ready in a flash!
—*D. Boutté*

Camera-Ready Cabbage Cleanse

Ingredients:

1 large head of green cabbage
1 pound carrots, peeled and chopped
1 (14.5-ounce) can diced fire-roasted tomatoes
1 (14.4-ounce) bag frozen French-cut green beans
2 cups chopped yellow onion
2 cups chopped celery
2 cups fresh chopped kale, stems removed
1 cup green bell pepper, cored, seeded and chopped
1 cup sliced green onions
3 tablespoons minced garlic
6 cups organic chicken stock
2 tablespoons Weeziana Girl Low Sodium Seasoning
2 tablespoons garlic powder
1 rotisserie chicken, deboned
Chicken bouillon (optional)

Directions:

- When it comes to this soup, the order of ingredients is irrelevant, so get your chop on and add to slow cooker as you go: cabbage, carrots, diced tomatoes, green beans, onions, celery, kale, bell pepper, green onions, garlic and 5 cups of chicken stock.
- Stir in Weeziana Girl and garlic powder. Cover.
- Remove rotisserie chicken from bones. Chop into bite-size chunks and add to cooker.
- Stir occasionally. Total cook time is 6–8 hours on low heat.
- When one hour of cook time remains, add any remaining stock and optional bouillon to achieve desired thickness and flavor.
- Eat as much as you want, whenever you want, for at least 1 week. The more you eat, the more your body will transform!

SUPER SALADS

Your body is your temple. Treat it as such. (photo taken by John Ganun)

Fast, filling and packed with flavor, these Super Salads are satisfying, healthy, easy to assemble and cost-effective. Say goodbye to boring, bland salads and experience a healthy, guilty pleasure.

**Incorporate these four tips and take your
salad game Out of the Stratosphere!**

1. Add life to your leafy greens by rinsing under cold water, shaking off excess moisture and stacking into a paper towel–lined storage bag or container. Seal and enjoy for weeks to come!

2. Go ,nuts! Adding the likes of walnuts, almonds and pecans will amplify texture and flavor while providing necessary protein.

3. The best dressings are homemade! The ones featured in this lineup will have you wondering why you ever bothered with the premade stuff. You can thank me later ;-)

4. Top with rotisserie chicken or my "Sesame Seared Shrimp" (see "Main Course" section) and make it a meal!

Nothing says "You're special" or "I love you" like carving time from your busy schedule, to prepare the perfect dish.
                                          —D. Boutté

Sesame Mardi Gras Slaw with Rotisserie Chicken

Ingredients:

Salad
4 cups shredded green cabbage
1 cup shredded purple cabbage
1 cup sliced green onions
3 tablespoons toasted sesame seeds
1 (4-ounce) package sliced almonds, toasted
Rotisserie chicken (optional)

Dressing
1/2 cup toasted sesame oil
4 1/2 tablespoons seasoned rice vinegar
1 tablespoon Weeziana Girl Low Sodium Seasoning
4 tablespoons sugar (or 1 1/2 teaspoons stevia)
1/2 teaspoon cracked black pepper

Directions:

- If almonds are raw, preheat oven to 350 degrees F and spread in single layer on baking sheet. Stir after 5 minutes, baking for total of 7-10 minutes. Cool.
- Shred then toss green and purple cabbage. Add sliced green onions. Refrigerate.
- Prepare dressing by adding sesame oil, rice vinegar, Weeziana Girl, sugar (or stevia) and black pepper.
- When time to *manger* (eat) add desired amount of dressing, sesame seeds and almonds to cooled salad. Toss.
- Top with chopped rotisserie chicken or enjoy the Flavor Disco vegetarian style!

Weeziana Girl Low Sodium Seasoning—
heart healthy and taste bud happy ☺
—D. Boutté

Savory Field Greens with Goat Cheese and Candied Pecans

Ingredients:

Salad
6 cups ready-to-eat spring/baby spinach mix
3 hard-boiled eggs, sliced
1 avocado, sliced
2 tablespoons fresh lemon juice
1/4 teaspoon Weeziana Girl Low Sodium Seasoning
1/4 teaspoon garlic powder
1/3 cup crumbled goat cheese
1/2 cup candied pecans, roughly chopped

Dressing
1/2 cup sugar (or stevia)
1/2 cup extra virgin olive oil
1/4 cup distilled white vinegar
1 teaspoon Weeziana Girl Low Sodium Seasoning
1/3 cup ketchup
2 tablespoons Worcestershire sauce
3 tablespoons grated yellow onion

Optional Toppings
1/4 cup dried cranberries
Sesame Seared Shrimp (see "Show-Stopping Main Courses")

Directions:

- Hard boil eggs.
- In small saucepan, combine sugar, olive oil, vinegar, Weeziana Girl, ketchup, Worcestershire sauce and yellow onion. Heat on low until sugar is dissolved, approximately 7 minutes. Set aside.
- Pit and slice avocado. Squeeze on lemon juice to prevent browning and sprinkle with Weeziana Girl and garlic powder.
- Add pecans. Save time and pick up a tasty bag that's ready to go!
- Peel and slice egg.
- Place desired amount of spring/spinach mix onto chilled plates.
- Layer on seasoned avocado, sliced egg, goat cheese crumbles, pecans and drizzle with desired amount of dressing.
- Wanna pack on even more flavor? Top with dried cranberries and/ or Sesame Seared Shrimp!

Kale Salad with Peanut Vinaigrette

Ingredients:

Salad

3 cups chopped kale
1 1/2 cups finely shredded green cabbage
5 finely chopped mint leaves
1 tablespoon lightly dried cilantro leaves
1/2 cup sliced green onion
1/2 cup salted roasted peanuts, chopped
Rotisserie chicken (optional)

Dressing

1/2 cup peanut oil
2 tablespoons toasted sesame oil
1/4 cup seasoned rice vinegar
1 tablespoon soy sauce
1 1/2 tablespoons honey
1 teaspoon minced garlic
2 tablespoons lemon juice
1/2 teaspoon cracked black pepper
Weeziana Girl Low Sodium Seasoning, to taste

Directions:

- Chop then add kale, cabbage, mint, cilantro and green onions to salad bowl. Cover and refrigerate as you prepare dressing.
- Add peanut and sesame oils, rice vinegar, soy sauce, honey, garlic, lemon juice, black pepper and Weeziana Girl to taste.
- When ready to eat, add desired amount of dressing, chopped peanuts and optional chicken. Toss and enjoy!

FEATURED EXTRAS...
SNACKS!

Mardi Gras time in Grand Marais, Louisiana

Whether you're looking for a satisfying appetizer or small bite for snacking, being short on time doesn't mean you need to indulge in mindless, unhealthy consumption. Every bite counts, folks! The act of eating is to be relished, to be savored, to nurture, to nourish. So go ahead... Enjoy even the simplest acts of eating and properly feed your Body, Mind and Spirit.

Chili Avocado Salmon Stacks

Ingredients:

1 bag crostini
1 tablespoon Weeziana Girl Low Sodium Seasoning, divided
1/2 cup Vegenaise (or mayonnaise)
2 tablespoons hot chili paste
1 avocado pitted, peeled and sliced
2 tablespoons fresh lemon juice
1 teaspoon garlic powder
8 slices crisp cooked bacon
12 ounces smoked salmon
4 hard boiled eggs, sliced
Freshly ground black pepper, to taste

Directions:

- If you can't find crostini toasted and ready to go, grab a French baguette from your local grocer, slice 1/4 inch thick and toast in a 350 degrees F oven for 15 minutes.
- Make spread by combining 1 teaspoon Weeziana Girl, vegenaise and chili paste.
- Pit and slice avocado. Squeeze on lemon juice to prevent browning and sprinkle with remaining Weeziana Girl and garlic powder.
- Cut each slice of bacon into 3 pieces.
- Get your stack on! Bottom up: crostini, chili spread, smoked salmon, seasoned avocado, bacon, egg slice and freshly cracked black pepper.

Weeziana Girl's Krunchy Kale Chips

Ingredients:

2 large bunches curly kale, rinsed and dried
2 tablespoons extra virgin olive oil
1 1/2 teaspoons Weeziana Girl Low Sodium Seasoning
1 teaspoon garlic powder

Directions:

- Preheat oven to 350°
- Remove kale stems, tear leaves into 2 inch pieces and place in bowl, large enough for tossing.
- Add olive oil, Weeziana Girl and garlic powder.
- Toss with hands until well coated.
- Arrange evenly onto foil-lined baking pan.
- Bake for 15 minutes. Toss gingerly. Return to oven.
- Check chips in 10-minute intervals, tossing gingerly between each. Will take 30 minutes to 1 hour of total cook time to achieve ultimate crunch!
- Enjoy while they last ;-)

Healthier choices don't mean deprivation or neglect. A small substitution can satisfy even the most discriminating of palates.
—D. Boutté

<u>Strawberry Raspberry Nice Cream</u>

Ingredients:

3 frozen bananas
1 cup frozen strawberries
1/2 cup frozen raspberries
3 tablespoons honey
1/2 cup Greek yogurt
1 cup coconut milk
1/3 cup granola of choice

Directions:

- Keep in mind that frozen banana will initially resemble the texture of oatmeal, but as it blends, will smooth out into a creamy, soft serve type texture.
- With exception of granola, toss all ingredients into blender and blend on high until smooth, approximately 2 minutes.
- Enjoy immediately (or freeze overnight if you prefer a firmer texture).
- Top with granola, extra berries and *Voila*!

Fresh Fruity Pops

Ingredients:

1/2 cup sliced strawberries
1/3 cup sliced kiwi
1/3 cup diced mangoes
1/3 cup blueberries
1/4 cup honey
1 cup (depends on size of mold) coconut water

Directions:

- Add all sliced and diced fruit, blueberries and honey to large bowl.
- Gently mix.
- Spoon fruit into popsicle molds (yields six 3-ounce pops).
- Pour coconut water to fill line.
- Freeze overnight. Enjoy tomorrow.

SHOW-STOPPING MAIN COURSES

Weeziana Girl Low Sodium Seasoning... She's Ready for Her Closeup!

When your Weeziana Girl is on a mission to tantalize those taste buds while keeping that hourglass figure in check, I break out this main-course arsenal. Each dish is packed with an array of flavor and is sure to leave an impression your guests won't soon forget. Pull out the "big guns" and show 'em what you're workin' with!

Sesame Seared Shrimp

Ingredients:

1 pound medium shrimp
1 1/2 tablespoons Weeziana Girl Low Sodium Seasoning
1 teaspoon garlic powder
1 teaspoon honey
1/4 teaspoon cracked black pepper
1 teaspoon fresh lime juice
2 tablespoons toasted sesame oil, divided
1 1/2 tablespoons vegan butter

Directions:

- Peel and devein shrimp. Rinse with cool water and pat dry with paper towel. Removing excess liquid will enhance searing process ;-)
- In separate bowl, whisk together Weeziana Girl, garlic powder, honey, black pepper, lime juice and 1 tablespoon sesame oil. Add shrimp.
- Cover and place in fridge for 15 minutes to marinate.
- Heat vegan butter in large frying pan over medium-high heat. Once hot, add shrimp in a single layer and sauté for 5–10 minutes, stirring occasionally. Don't be afraid of sizzle! If necessary, add 1 tablespoon of water to deglaze, releasing stuck-on goodness from pan.
- When 1 minute of cook time remains, add remaining sesame oil.
- Serve alone or as topping for a slew of tasty dishes!

Pasta d'Asperges

Ingredients:

1 pound fresh asparagus
1 tablespoon sea salt
1/4 cup extra virgin olive oil, divided
1 pound gluten-free penne, mafalda, or preferred pasta
1 tablespoon vegan butter
1 medium zucchini
1 1/2 cups chopped yellow onion
1 (14.5-ounce) can diced basil, garlic, oregano tomatoes
1 teaspoon fresh grated lemon zest
Weeziana Girl Low Sodium Seasoning, to taste
1/3 cup freshly grated parmesan cheese (optional)

Directions:

- Cut asparagus into 1-inch pieces, setting aside tips and discarding tough ends.
- In large pot, bring 5 quarts of salted water to boil. Add asparagus stems and boil until tender about 7 minutes, depending on thickness of stalks.
- Using slotted spoon, remove from pot. Set aside.
- To same pot, add asparagus tips and cook until al dente, about 5 minutes. Again, using slotted spoon, remove from pot. Set aside.
- Once again using same pot, add 1 tablespoon of olive oil and boil pasta for 3/4 of recommended cook time; not yet al dente. Remove from pot and set aside. Turn off and reserve water.
- Peel zucchini, cut in half lengthwise and slice into 1/4-inch pieces.
- In Dutch oven, sauté zucchini and onion in butter over medium-high heat. Once onions are clear and browning has occurred (about 7 minutes), add diced tomato and simmer. Stir occasionally, adding salted water, as needed to maintain desired consistency.
- While sauce cooks, puree asparagus stems with lemon zest, remaining olive oil and 1/3 cup asparagus cooking water. Add to sauce.
- Add cooked pasta, additional cup of reserved water and Weeziana Girl to taste. Simmer for 5–7 minutes, stirring occasionally.
- Once pasta is al dente, stir in reserved asparagus tips.
- Top with freshly grated parmesan cheese.

Grilled Honey-Sesame Marinated Chicken

Ingredients:

4 (8-ounce) bone-in chicken thighs
2 tablespoons apple cider vinegar
1/3 cup low-sodium soy sauce
3 tablespoons honey
2 tablespoons toasted sesame oil
3 fresh rosemary sprigs
1 tablespoon Weeziana Girl Low Sodium Seasoning
1 tablespoon minced garlic

Directions:

- Rinse chicken thighs under cool water. Pat dry with paper towel.
- In bowl, whisk together remaining ingredients: vinegar, soy sauce, honey, sesame oil, rosemary, Weeziana Girl and garlic.
- Set aside 1/4 cup of marinade (this will be used to baste chicken while grilling).
- Pour rest of marinade into large zipper bag, removing as much air possible. Add chicken and allow to marinate in fridge for 2–3 hours.
- Heat grill to medium heat.
- Remove chicken from fridge, discarding rosemary sprigs.
- Transfer chicken from marinade to grill. Cook thighs for approximately 5–10 minutes on each side, brushing liberally with reserved marinade.
- Cook until skin is crisp and meat is seared. Internal temperature should read 160 degrees F when thermometer is inserted into thickest part of meat.
- Bon appétit!

Chilean "Tea" Bass over Sautéed Spinach

Ingredients:

Chilean Sea Bass
2 1/2 pounds Chilean sea bass fillets
1 1/2 cups water
2/3 cup low-sodium soy sauce
1/2 cup organic brown sugar
1 tablespoon Weeziana Girl Low Sodium Seasoning
2 teaspoons fresh ginger, peeled and grated
1 teaspoon minced garlic
1 bag oolong tea

Spinach
10 ounces ready-to-eat baby spinach
1 tablespoon vegan butter
1 tablespoon extra virgin olive oil
1 teaspoon minced garlic
1/2 teaspoon Weeziana Girl Low Sodium Seasoning
Freshly ground black pepper

Directions:

- In a small saucepan, combine water, soy sauce, brown sugar, Weeziana Girl, ginger and garlic. Bring to a boil over medium-high heat. Add tea bag, then reduce to low simmer for 5 minutes. Remove tea bag. Cool.
- Rinse sea bass fillets under cool water. Pat dry with paper towels.
- Pour 2 cups marinade into large zipper bag, add sea bass and seal, removing as much air possible. Reserve remaining marinade for cooking.
- Marinade in fridge for 5–7 hours.
- Once marinade process is complete, preheat oven to 425 degrees F.
- Place fillets onto parchment-lined baking pan and bake for 20 minutes. Brush liberally throughout cook time with leftover marinade.
- About 10 minutes after fillets begin to bake, in a large skillet, add garlic to melted butter and olive oil. Cook for 3 minutes, until softened.
- Add spinach, one handful at a time.
- Toss, seasoning with Weeziana Girl and black pepper to taste. After 3–5 minutes, "Project Spinach Wilt" is complete.
- Once edges of fish begin browning, turn oven up to broil and cook for another 3–5 minutes, watching closely. Remove from oven, once dark patches develop around fillet edges.
- Use tongs to place spinach in center of plate.
- Use spatula to carefully nestle each fillet onto bed of spinach.
- Any remaining sauce should be drizzled atop each fillet.
- Let it "melt in your mouth."
- Warning! Preparing this dish, may prompt a proposal ;-)

Hoisin and Ginger Glazed Salmon

Ingredients:

1 boneless, skin-on salmon filet (1 1/2 to 2 pounds)
2 tablespoons toasted sesame oil
2 tablespoons fresh lemon juice
1/3 cup low-sodium soy sauce
1/4 cup hoisin sauce
1 tablespoon hot chili sauce
1 tablespoon fresh ginger, peeled and grated
2 tablespoons grated onion
1 tablespoon minced garlic
1 tablespoon parsley paste
1 tablespoon Weeziana Girl Low Sodium Seasoning

Directions:

- To saucepan, add sesame oil, fresh squeezed lemon juice, soy, hoisin and chili sauce. The order in which you add is irrelevant, so just go for it!
- Whisk in ginger, onion, garlic, parsley paste and Weeziana Girl. Simmer over low heat for 10 minutes. Cool.
- Pour glaze into large, sealable bag or covered dish, to evenly coat.
- Add salmon, skin up, into marinade. Place in refrigerator for minimum of 30 minutes.
- Preheat oven to 350 degrees F.
- Remove fish from fridge and place (flesh side, up) onto a shallow baking pan. Baste throughout cook time with remaining sauce.
- Cooking time varies depending on thickness of fish, but typically 20–30 minutes yields perfection.

SCENE-STEALING VEGGIES

The Maurice Head Start years. Love to the original 4... Mrs. Jane, Ms. Pearl, Mrs. Brenda & Momma Betty!

Eating your vegetables is meant to be a Blessing, not a curse! When old-school favorites get new-school updates, you breathe new life into items that have become boring or bland. Open yourself to experimenting with new ingredients and exploring the unexpected, especially when it comes to the vast world of veggies. Play with your food—I dare ya!

Zydeco Shuffle

Ingredients:

1/2 cup chicken stock
Pinch sea salt (optional)
1 1/2 pounds fresh green beans, washed and trimmed
1 tablespoon extra-virgin olive oil
2 cups yellow onions, thinly sliced
1/2 cup cored, seeded and chopped red bell pepper
2 tablespoons minced garlic
2 teaspoons Weeziana Girl Low Sodium Seasoning
1 teaspoon garlic powder
1/2 cup sliced green onions
1 1/2 teaspoons parsley paste
1 tablespoon toasted sesame oil

Directions:

- In large pot, bring chicken stock and optional sea salt to a boil.
- Once boiling, add green beans. Boil, covered, for 6 minutes (stirring halfway through), until slightly tender. Set aside, uncovered.
- In heavy-bottom Dutch oven, heat olive oil over medium-high heat. Add onion, bell pepper, garlic, 1 teaspoon Weeziana Girl and garlic powder. Sauté 10 minutes. Deglaze any caramelized bits using remaining stock from boiled green beans.
- Add green beans to Dutch oven, along with remaining Weeziana Girl, green onions and parsley paste. Mix well and cook 5 minutes more.
- When one minute of cook time remains, add sesame oil. Enjoy while hot.

Corn Macque Choux

Ingredients:

8 ears shucked fresh corn

2 tablespoons extra-virgin olive oil

1 cup diced yellow onions

1/2 cup cored, seeded and chopped green bell pepper

2 tablespoons minced garlic

1 tablespoon Weeziana Girl Low Sodium Seasoning

1 tablespoon vegan butter

1/2 cup chicken stock

2 tablespoons tomato sauce

1 (14.5-ounce) can diced fire-roasted tomatoes

1/2 cup sliced green onions

1/4 cup fresh chopped parsley

1 teaspoon garlic powder

1 packet (2 grams) stevia

1 pound medium shrimp (optional)

Directions:

- Using a sharp knife, cut corn kernels lengthwise from cob, into large bowl. Scrape downward to remove additional pulp and juice. Set aside.
- In Dutch oven, heat olive oil over medium-high heat. Add onions, bell pepper, garlic and 1 teaspoon of Weeziana Girl. Sauté 7 minutes.
- Add corn and vegan butter. Cook for an additional 15 minutes.
- Stir in chicken stock, tomato sauce, roasted tomatoes, green onions, fresh parsley, garlic powder, stevia and remaining Weeziana Girl. If using shrimp, now is the time to add.
- Reduce heat to medium-low and simmer for 20 minutes, allowing dish to thicken and flavors to tango.

Cheesy Spinach and Garlic Orangetti Squash

Ingredients:

1 large orangetti or spaghetti squash
2 teaspoons extra virgin olive oil
1 teaspoon ground black pepper
1 tablespoon vegan butter
1/2 cup chopped red onion
2 tablespoons minced garlic
3 cups fresh chopped spinach
1 1/2 teaspoons parsley paste

1/2 cup whole milk
1 tablespoon Weeziana Girl Low Sodium Seasoning
1 teaspoon garlic powder
1/3 cup fresh grated parmesan cheese
1/2 cup chopped rotisserie chicken (optional)

Directions:

- Preheat oven to 400 degrees F.
- Cut squash in half, lengthwise and scoop out pulp and seeds.
- Using foil, create small circular rings that each half can sit upon in baking pan, stabilizing liquids and squash as it softens and cooks.
- Brush 1/2 teaspoon of olive oil onto each half and sprinkle with black pepper.
- In large skillet, heat remaining olive oil and vegan butter. Add then sauté onion, garlic and chopped spinach. Cook for 5–7 minutes until softened and most liquid has evaporated.
- Stir in parsley paste, milk, Weeziana Girl and garlic powder.
- Directly into squash halves, sprinkle grated Parmesan cheese. If using rotisserie chicken, this is the perfect time to add that punch of protein.
- Fill cavity of each squash with spinach/milk sauté.
- Carefully place in oven. Roast for 30 minutes.
- When you remove from oven, flesh of squash should be tender enough to separate strands from skin using a fork.
- Mix well and return to oven. Cook for an additional 20 minutes.
- Enjoy while it's hot!

VIP SMOOTHIES

It's cooking demo time. Bon Appétit!

Perfect for kickin' off your morning, peppin' up your mid-day or toppin' off your night… ANY time's the right time for a Slammin' Smoothie. As long as you're using ingredients and flavors you love, you can't mess this stuff up! I'll always slide in frozen bananas for the perfect silky texture, veggies to ensure I get in my daily dose, boosts like chia seeds, flax, acai or hemp that'll enhance the health factor, and ice to enhance girth. Remember—every meal counts. Make the most of it!

Orange Radiance

Ingredients:

2 cups frozen mango chunks
1 cup orange juice
1 cup carrots, cut into chunks or
    use baby carrots
1 frozen banana

1 tablespoon fresh lime juice
1 cup Greek yogurt
1 cup soy milk
1 cup ice

Boost of Choice: Ground flax seeds

Place all ingredients into container and blend on high until smooth, approximately 30 seconds. Serve immediately.

Lotta Colada

Ingredients:

1 cup fresh pineapple chunks
2/3 cup toasted coconut Greek
    yogurt
1 frozen banana

1/2 cup vanilla coconut milk
1/2 cup whole grain oatmeal
2 teaspoons honey
1 cup ice

Boost of Choice: Chia and ground flax seeds

Place all ingredients into container and blend on high until smooth, approximately 30 seconds. Serve immediately.

Purple Serenity

Ingredients:

1 cup frozen strawberries
1 cup vanilla almond milk
1 frozen banana
1/2 cup ice

3/4 cup fresh beets, peeled and
    chunked
1/2 cup frozen blueberries
1/2 cup pomegranate juice

Boost of Choice: Acai powder

Place all ingredients into container and blend on high until smooth, approximately 30 seconds. Serve immediately.

Peach Pastry

Ingredients:

1 1/2 cups vanilla almond milk
1/2 cup Greek yogurt
1 1/2 cups frozen peaches
6 dried apricots, chopped
1 tablespoon honey

1 teaspoon natural vanilla extract
1/4 teaspoon ground cinnamon
Pinch fresh ground nutmeg
Pinch fresh ginger, peeled and grated

Boost of Choice: Chia seeds

Place all ingredients into container and blend on high until smooth, approximately 30 seconds. Serve immediately.

Allana's Faithful Fuel-Up

Ingredients:

2 frozen bananas
1/2 cup carrots, cut into chunks or
    use baby carrots
2 cups coconut milk
1 sweet apple (I prefer pink lady
    or honey crisp) cored, seeded
    and chopped

3/4 cup fresh beets, peeled and
    chunked
1 1/2 teaspoons fresh ginger, peeled
    and grated
1 cup ice

Boost of Choice: Chia seeds

Place all ingredients into container and blend on high until smooth, approximately 30 seconds. Serve immediately.

Green Goddess with Ginger

Ingredients:

2 dates, pitted and softened
1 cup fresh chopped kale, stems
    removed
1/4 cup packed baby spinach
1 tablespoon fresh ginger, peeled
    and grated

1 cup pineapple chunks
1 frozen banana
1 cup vanilla almond milk
1/4 cup water
1 cup ice

Boost of Choice: Hemp powder

If time allows, soften dates by soaking in 1/4 cup of water for 20 minutes. Place all ingredients (including water used to soak dates) into container and blend on high until smooth, approximately 30 seconds. Serve immediately.

<u>Sweet Potato Sunset</u>

Ingredients:

1 medium sweet potato, baked
1 frozen banana
1 tablespoon almond butter
1 1/2 cups almond milk
2 tablespoons agave nectar

1 teaspoon fresh, chopped ginger
1/4 teaspoon cinnamon
1/4 teaspoon ground turmeric
1 cup ice

Boost of Choice: Ground flax seeds

Strongly encourage planning ahead and cooking multiple sweet potatoes, as they should be baked to maximize flavor. Prick with fork, bake at 400 degrees F until soft, approximately 30 minutes. Once cooled, scoop from skin, add to container with all other ingredients and blend on high until smooth, approximately 30 seconds. Serve immediately.

A WORD OF THANKS

First and foremost, I thank the Most High for allowing the faithful mustard seed I planted over a dozen years ago, to bear such beautiful fruit !

I could never have done this without the unwavering support and encouragement of my best friend and husband Kevin and inspiration of our eternal sunshine, Jordan. You inspire me. Because of you, I have a firm foundation upon which I can build, evolve and continue to dream.

Countless Family and Friends to thank but I'll keep it brief. To my "brother from another mother" and fellow Louisiana native, Tyler Perry... Thanks for going beyond the resume, recognizing raw talent and providing a safe environment in which to learn, grow and thrive. Love to my Manager and dear friend Charles; your unwavering support and light keep my spirit on positive. To Chef Jernard for joining forces with me on this *Modified* journey and gratitude to my big brother Brian, for embarking with me on this Weeziana Girl adventure. To Momma Betty for nurturing my core, to Mon Mon and PaPa for fueling my drive and passion. My Village may be small, but it sure is Mighty! To you, I am beyond grateful for constant Love, Prayer and Support. You are the authentic reflection, of how Blessed I truly am.

XoXo –
Your Weeziana Girl,

D. Boutte

Jernard and Keena Wells out on a date

Note from The Chef of Love

Being known as the Chef of Love, my true goal in life has always been to help the viewer and reader understand that food has always played a significant role in our life. Whatever the occasion is, be it a celebration of love, marriage, birthday parties, promotions, or just Sunday gatherings, food is one of the many keys to the heart. Food is the international language. I've never seen a person eating and frowning! Great meals keep us coming back for more. My philosophy is that food is about bringing people into our world. We truly cook from the heart. Two people can cook the same meal following the same recipe and it can taste completely different. Food is truly tied to our soul, and that's where we should always strive to cook from. I live by the 4Fs: faith, family, food, and fun.

Unlock a great recipe and you will unlock someone's heart.

Jernard Wells

Jernard and Keena Wells spending quality time together

Acknowledgment

My thanks to God foremost. To my wife, Keena, and our children, Carleisha, Jamia, Jalisa, Jernard Jr., Kameron, Keenan, and Jacobe. To Jasmine and Zoe who are my soul's inspiration, my close friends who stood by me and behind me from start to finish—not to mention countless experimental dinners and taste tests.

My motivation from within has come from countless years of wanting to prepare meals that would make my guests smile through the aromas and tastes of lovingly prepared food. I show my love through the good food that I prepare, because I strongly believe that one of the pathways to any individual's heart is through great food.

There are many colleagues from whom I have learned from during my endeavors preparing meals, but I would like to give a special mention to friends and lovely family members who have directly contributed ideas to me, especially my mother, Gwendolyn Willis, and my sisters Towonda, Shannon, Latonya, Marquita, and Mary, and my brothers Adam, Anthony, and Lester. I want to give a big thanks to my close friends, PR marketing executive Carlos Scott, Sous Chef Cory Hinton and my communication director Mia Lloyd, for helping the world see my light.

Jernard Wells

The Chef of Love

Growing up in the South, we had access to all kinds of fresh-grown vegetables and herbs. Butternut Squash is a vegetable you can prepare so many different ways and get a unique experience every time—sautéed, baked, roasted, you name it.

Roasted Butternut Squash and Spinach (VEGAN)

Ingredients:	Directions:
2 medium butternut squash 2 tablespoons olive oil 1 teaspoon olive oil Kosher salt and pepper 1/4 cup sliced peanuts 1/4 teaspoon ground cinnamon 1 pinch cayenne pepper 3 cups baby spinach	Heat oven to 425 degrees F. On a large rimmed baking sheet, toss butternut squash with 2 tablespoons oil and 1/2 teaspoon each salt and pepper. Roast for 20 minutes. Meanwhile, in a small bowl, toss the almonds with the remaining teaspoon oil, then the cinnamon and cayenne. Scatter the peanuts over the squash and continue roasting until the almonds are golden brown and the squash is tender, about 5 minutes more. Scatter the spinach over the squash and almonds and let sit for 1 minute, then gently fold together.

Chardonnay Beans and Tomatoes (VEGAN)

Ingredients:	Directions:
1 tablespoon sesame oil 2 cloves garlic, minced 1 pint and small cherry or grape tomatoes 1/2 sprig fresh rosemary 1/4 cup chardonnay wine 1 can cannellini beans Kosher salt pepper 1/4 cup chopped fresh flat-leaf parsley	Heat the oil in a large skillet over medium heat. Add the garlic and cook, stirring occasionally, until beginning to brown, about 2 minutes. Add the tomatoes and rosemary and cook, stirring, for 1 minute. Add the wine and bring to a simmer. Stir in the beans and 1/2 teaspoon each salt and pepper and cook until heated through, about 1 minute more. Toss with parsley.

Smokey Chickpea Pepper Soup with Quinoa (VEGAN)

Ingredients:	Directions:
1/2 cup quinoa 2 tablespoons olive oil 1 medium sweet onion, diced 1 carrot, diced 1 stalk celery, diced 2 clove garlic, minced 2 tablespoons minced smoked chipotle Kosher salt pepper 1 yellow bell pepper, diced 1 red bell pepper, diced 1 small can chickpeas 2 cup low-sodium vegetable broth 2 tablespoons balsamic vinegar 1 cup cooked quinoa chopped fresh parsley	Cook the quinoa according to package directions. Meanwhile, heat the oil in a Dutch oven or large heavy-bottomed pot. Add the onion, carrot, and celery and cook, covered, stirring occasionally, 6 minutes. Add garlic, chipotle, and 1/4 teaspoon each salt and pepper and cook, stirring, 1 minute. Add peppers and cook, stirring occasionally, 5 minutes. Add the chickpeas, broth, and 1 cup water and bring to a boil. Reduce heat and simmer until the vegetables are tender, 5–8 minutes. Stir in balsamic vinegar and cooked quinoa. Serve topped with parsley, if desired.

Micro greens pack a lot of nutrients and flavor. Growing up in Mississippi, my father would always feed me watercress. It became my first love, before iceberg lettuce. Creating this dish with a touch of Asian flare gives it a bold flavor beyond your average salad.

Sesame Micro Green Salad (VEGAN)

Ingredients:	Directions:
3 bunches watercress 2 bunch micro greens 2 stalk celery, diced 1/2 cup coarsely chopped roasted salted peanuts 2 tablespoons toasted sesame oil 2 tablespoons seasoned rice wine vinegar 1 tablespoon soy sauce 1 teaspoon Thai chili-garlic sauce 2 tablespoons sesame seeds	In a large bowl, combine micro greens, watercress, celery, and peanuts. In a small bowl, whisk sesame oil, vinegar, soy sauce, and Thai chili-garlic sauce to combine. Toss greens with dressing to coat. Divide dressed salad among plates and sprinkle with sesame seeds.

When I was young, Brussels sprouts were never on my list to eat, but as I got older, it became one of my most flavorful and favorite dishes, especially when prepared with lemon pepper and parmesan.

Lemon Parmesan Roasted Brussels Sprouts (Vegetarian)

Ingredients:	Directions:
1 1/2 pounds Brussels sprouts, ends trimmed, halved 3 tablespoons olive oil 3 tablespoons grated parmesan 1 tablespoon honey 2 tablespoons lemon zest 1 teaspoon kosher salt 1/2 teaspoon freshly ground black pepper	Preheat oven to 400 degrees F. Place Brussels sprouts, olive oil, kosher salt, honey, and pepper in a medium bowl. Shake to coat. Pour onto a baking sheet and place on the oven's center rack. Roast in preheated oven for 25–35 minutes, shaking pan every 5 to 7 minutes to ensure even browning. Reduce heat when necessary to prevent burning. Brussels sprouts should be darkest brown, almost black, when done. Adjust seasoning with kosher salt and sprinkle with parmesan and lemon zest. Serve immediately.

Roasted Tomato Eggplant Parmesan (Vegetarian)

Ingredients:	Directions:
3 eggplants, peeled and thinly sliced 2 eggs, beaten 3 cups Italian seasoned bread crumbs 4 (10-ounce) cans diced fire roasted tomatoes, in juice, for sauce, divided 1 (16-ounce) package mozzarella cheese, shredded and divided 1/2 cup grated parmesan cheese, divided 1 bunch of fresh basil, minced	Preheat oven to 350 degrees F. Dip eggplant slices in egg, then in bread crumbs. Place in a single layer on a baking sheet. Bake in preheated oven for 5 minutes on each side. In a 9-inch x 13-inch baking dish, spread roasted diced tomatoes to cover the bottom. Place a layer of eggplant slices in the sauce. Sprinkle with mozzarella and parmesan cheeses. Repeat with remaining ingredients, ending with the cheeses. Sprinkle basil on top. Bake in preheated oven for 35 minutes, or until golden. Brown.

I love spaghetti and I love squash. When I bring the two together it's a match made in heaven.

Spaghetti Squash with Basil Marinara (Vegetarian)

Ingredients:	Directions:
2 spaghetti squash 1/4 cup extra-virgin olive oil Sea salt and freshly ground black pepper 1 bunch of fresh basil 1 tablespoon brown sugar 4 cups marinara sauce	Preheat oven to 450 degrees F. Split the squashes in half and scrape out seeds. Line an oven tray with aluminum foil. Season spaghetti squash with olive oil, salt, and pepper. Place flesh side down and roast 30–40 minutes, until fully cooked. Remove from oven and let rest until cool enough to handle. Heat marinara sauce in a large sauté pan. Add brown sugar, basil, and salt and pepper to taste. When squash is cool enough to handle, using a large kitchen spoon, scrape the strands of squash from the inside of the skin. Toss the squash in the pan with the basil and marinara enough until everything is hot. Serve and enjoy.

Gouda cheese dates from the year 1184, making it one of the oldest recorded cheeses in the world still made today. One of the most popular cheeses and one of the best, I might add, it has a unique smoky flavor and is magnificent on baked potatoes.

Smoked Gouda and Poblano Twice-Baked Potatoes (Vegetarian)

Ingredients:	Directions:
6 medium-size red potatoes 1 fresh poblano, seeded and diced 1 tablespoon butter 1/4 cup light sour cream 1/4 teaspoon salt 1/4 teaspoon pepper 1 cup smoked gouda cheese, divided	Preheat oven to 375 degrees F. Wash potatoes and wrap tightly in aluminum foil. Bake 45 minutes or until softened. Remove potatoes from oven and unwrap. Slice each potato in half and carefully scoop out inside, trying not to puncture skin. Spray muffin tin with cooking spray and place a hollowed-out potato in each muffin tin. Set aside. In a medium bowl, combine scooped-out potato with diced poblano, butter, sour cream, salt, pepper and 1/2 cup of smoked gouda cheese. Stir until combined. Spoon mixture back into potato skins. Top with remaining 1/2 cup gouda cheese. Bake for 25–30 minutes, until skins are crisp and cheese is melted

Two of my favorite dishes are fajitas and sweet potatoes. This is my own version of a loaded bake potato, but with so much more.

Twice-Baked Fajita Sweet Potatoes (Vegetarian)

Ingredients:	Directions:
3 whole medium sweet potatoes, washed and scrubbed Olive oil 1/2 red onion, thinly sliced 1 tablespoon sea salt 1 tablespoon black pepper 1 clove garlic, minced 1 small red bell pepper, diced 1 small yellow bell pepper, diced 1 small green bell pepper, diced 1/4 cup canned black beans, washed and rinsed 1/2 teaspoon ground cumin 1 teaspoon smoked paprika 1 cup shredded Mexican cheese 1 lime, juiced 1/4 cup cilantro leaves Extra lime wedges to serve 1 avocado, diced	Wrap sweet potatoes in a piece of foil. Preheat oven and bake at 400 degrees F for 65 minutes. Remove carefully from oven and unwrap. While the sweet potatoes are cooking, add a small amount of oil to large skillet. Sauté onions over medium heat. Once transparent (about 1–2 minutes), add garlic and peppers. Cook until garlic is fragrant. Add cumin, paprika, black pepper, and salt and continue cooking. Mix beans through. Take off heat and set aside. Remove sweet potatoes from oven; allow to cool for about 5 minutes until they are just warm enough to handle and carefully slice in half. Slice around the inside of the skin. Slice small cubes into the flesh for easier removal. Scoop out the flesh and transfer it to a medium mixing bowl. Set the skins aside.

Add the fajita mixture to the flesh in the bowl; mix it through until completely combined. Stir in the lime juice.

Arrange the skins on the same baking tray and stuff them with the fajita sweet potato mixture. Sprinkle with cheese and cilantro leaves. Place back into the oven for 10 minutes until cheese is bubbling. Serve with cilantro leaves, lime wedges, and diced avocado.

Carrot, Pepper, Black Bean Tacos (Vegetarian)

Ingredients:	Directions:
3 tablespoons peanut oil or olive oil, divided 1 small onion, chopped 1 poblano pepper, diced 1 bell pepper, diced 1 teaspoon chipotle chili powder 1 (15.5-ounce) can black beans, drained and rinsed 1 tablespoon fresh lime juice, plus wedges for serving Kosher salt Freshly ground black pepper 1/2 pound medium carrots, cut into 3–4 inch sticks 1 teaspoon ground cumin 8 whole-grain taco shells, warmed 1/3 cup vegetable stock Sliced avocado 1/2 cup crumbled queso fresco 1/4 cup chopped fresh cilantro 2 radishes sliced thin	Preheat oven to 450 degrees F. Heat 1 1/2 tablespoons oil in a medium saucepan over medium heat. Add onion and peppers, stirring occasionally, until tender, 4 to 6 minutes. Add chipotle chili powder and cook, stirring until fragrant, 30 seconds. Add black beans and vegetable stock. Reduce heat and cook, stirring occasionally, until thickened, 4–6 minutes. Mash beans with back of spoon until thick. Stir in lime juice. Season with salt and pepper. Meanwhile, toss carrots with cumin and 1 1/2 tablespoons peanut oil place on baking sheet. Season with salt and pepper. Roast, turning once, until just tender, 15 minutes. Divide beans and carrots between taco shells. Top with avocado, queso, cilantro, and radishes.

Being a lover of all things barbecue, I discovered this amazing fruit one day while cruising through the aisles of my local farmers' market. What an amazing fruit it is. Jackfruit has the texture of pulled pork, and if you follow this recipe your guests will never know the difference.

Barbecue Pulled Jackfruit Sandwich (Vegetarian)

Ingredients:	Directions:
BBQ Jackfruit 2 pounds young green jackfruit 1/4 cup BBQ seasoning 1–2 tablespoons oil 3 tablespoons brown sugar 1 teaspoon paprika 1 teaspoon garlic powder 1/2 teaspoon salt 1/2 teaspoon pepper 1/2 teaspoon chili powder 3/4 cup BBQ sauce **Avocado Slaw (optional)** 2 cups shredded cabbage and carrots 1/2 ripe avocado sliced 1 tablespoon coconut sugar Juice of 1 lemon or lime Salt and pepper, to taste	Rinse, drain, and thoroughly dry jackfruit. Chop off the center "core" portion of the fruit and discard. Place in a mixing bowl and set aside. Mix together BBQ seasoning and add to jackfruit. Toss to coat. Heat a large skillet over medium heat. Once hot, add oil and seasoned jackfruit. Cook for 2–3 minutes. Add BBQ sauce. Stir and reduce heat to low- medium and cook for about 15 minutes on medium. Remove lid and stir occasionally. Use two forks to shred the jackfruit as it cooks down. Make slaw by adding all ingredients to a small mixing bowl and whisk to combine. Set in the refrigerator until serving. Once the jackfruit has been properly simmered, turn up heat to medium-high and cook for 2 more minutes to get a little shredded texture. Remove from heat. Place generous portions of BBQ jackfruit on the bottom buns. Top with slaw. Serve with BBQ sauce on side!

Jernard with his youngest daughters Jasmine and Zoe

Who doesn't love a good hot wing? It should be in everyone's recipe portfolio. Well, just because you want to eat healthy, that doesn't mean you should give up the good things that you love to eat! You can put a twist on it—bake it and make it better. That is what I have done with this mouthwatering coconut-baked wing. You get the same great flavor in a healthier dish that's guaranteed to make your taste buds jump for joy!

The hot wing has always been a tradition in our house. We have served them for games, celebrations, and any family gathering where we needed a quick finger food to appease the appetite quickly. Each bite packs a sweet one-of-a-kind bite, with the hint of coconut, which will melt in your mouth. Growing up, we didn't believe in baking wings, but this wing will have the adults and kids racing for a seat at the table.

Chef of Love's Oven-Roasted Coconut Hot Wings

Ingredients:

4–5 pounds chicken wings
4 tablespoons black pepper
Pinch of salt
1/4 cup coconut milk
1/2 cup Caribbean Island Fire
Sauce or other hot sauce
3 tablespoons coconut sugar
1 tablespoon cayenne pepper

Directions:

Preheat oven to 375 degrees F. Season wings with salt and pepper and layer on sheet pan. Bake in oven, uncovered, for 45–55 minutes, until golden and crispy in texture. Remove them and place on a paper towel to drain the grease. Heat coconut milk in a heavy saucepan. Add the Caribbean Island Fire Sauce or hot sauce and the other ingredients and stir. Bring to slow simmer and remove from heat. Place chicken in a bowl with lid, pour the sauce over the chicken, and shake very lightly. Cover the chicken for a few moments and serve. This meal is great served with celery or carrots and ranch or blue cheese sauce.

Chef Jernard smiling back at you

Growing up, I knew we were on the brink of summer when I would come home from school and smell fresh watermelon in the air. My mother and grandmother always had the table laid out and ready for dinner before the sun would set. They carefully selected the sweetest, freshest, ripest watermelons they could find, and it was a win every time. I looked forward to many dishes, such as fruit salads, side salads, or just plain watermelon served as a fresh sorbet.

In today's world, it is a special moment when we can fix something quick and refreshing that reminds us of our upbringing. This recipe will take you back but keep you healthy too! Fresh watermelon and fresh figs together in a salad makes for a perfect light starter to any great meal! This is a new formula for success to a great meal with fewer calories, and you never compromise on the taste.

Wet 'n' Wild Fig Watermelon Salad

Ingredients:	Directions:
3/4 cup thinly sliced red onions 2 tablespoons fresh lime juice 1 1/2 quarts seeded, cubed watermelon 3/4 cup crumbled feta cheese 1/2 cup pitted black olive halves 1/4 cup diced pitted figs 1 cup chopped fresh mint 5 tablespoons fig balsamic vinegar	Place the onion slices in a small bowl with the lime juice. The acid of the lime will mellow out the raw onions. Let stand for 12 minutes. In a large bowl, combine watermelon cubes, feta cheese, figs, black olives, and onions with the lime juice and mint. Drizzle fig balsamic oil over salad. Prepare for a pleasant surprise.

Smoked Chicken Salad Lettuce Cups

Ingredients:	Directions:
1/4 cup chopped walnuts 1/4 cup extra virgin olive oil mayonnaise 1/4 cup plain fat-free Greek yogurt 2 teaspoons liquid smoke 1/4 teaspoon kosher salt 1/4 teaspoon freshly ground black pepper 2 cups shredded skinless, boneless rotisserie chicken breast 2 tablespoons chopped fresh flat-leaf parsley 6 green onions, white and light green parts, chopped 6 Boston Bibb lettuce leaves Cherries (for serving)	Preheat oven to 350 degrees F. Spread walnuts in a single layer on a baking sheet; bake for 5 minutes or until nuts are toasted. Cool. Combine mayonnaise, yogurt, liquid smoke, sea salt, and pepper in a bowl; stir to combine. Set aside. Place chicken, toasted walnuts, parsley, and green onions in a large bowl; toss to combine. Add dressing, stirring well to coat. Place 1 lettuce leaf in each of 6 bowls. Divide chicken salad evenly among the bowls; top with cherries.

Mississippi Blackened Catfish Po'boys

Ingredients:

2 catfish fillets, approximately 2 pounds total
Blackening seasoning (recipe below)
2 teaspoons olive oil, divided
Sweet pickle remoulade (recipe below)
French baguette, sliced into 4-inch hunks
Optional garnish: fresh lemon, lettuce, sweet pickles

Blackening Seasoning

2 tablespoons smoked paprika
1/2 teaspoon salt
1/2 teaspoon black pepper
1/2 teaspoon garlic powder
1/2 teaspoon onion powder
1/2 teaspoon cayenne
1/2 teaspoon oregano

Sweet Pickle Remoulade

1/2 cup plain Yogurt
1/4 cup minced sweet pickles
1/4 teaspoon salt
1 teaspoon pickle juice
1/2 teaspoon hot sauce
2 teaspoons Dijon
2 teaspoons horseradish
1/2 teaspoon Worcestershire sauce

Directions:

Move the oven rack to its highest possible position. Preheat oven to broil. Line a baking sheet with foil. In a small bowl, combine the blackening seasoning.
In a separate small bowl, combine the sweet pickle remoulade ingredients, then refrigerate. Lightly coat each of the catfish fillets with 1/2 teaspoon olive oil per side. Rub each side of fillet with blackening seasoning. Place fillets on baking sheet and broil for 4–5 minutes per side, or until fish is flaky in the center.
Halve each catfish fillet and then place each half on a baguette. Finish with the sweet pickle remoulade sauce, a squeeze of fresh lemon, lettuce, and pickles, as desired.

No-Bread-Crumbs Crab Cakes

What's a crab cake without breadcrumbs, you might ask! Well, the inspiration to this recipe was to create a healthy alternative for crab cakes that would not alter the flavor that puts this Louisiana favorite at the top of every seafood lover's list!

Ingredients:	Directions:
For the Crab Cakes 1 tablespoon coconut oil 1/2 onion, finely chopped 2 stalks celery, finely chopped 1/2 large red bell pepper, finely chopped 1 bunch green onions (green portion only), chopped 1/2 large carrot, finely chopped 3 cloves garlic, minced 1 tablespoon parsley flakes 2 teaspoons Creole seasoning 2 teaspoons dried basil 2 teaspoons ground black pepper 1 teaspoon dried dill weed 1/2 teaspoon oregano 1/2 teaspoon dried thyme 2 large eggs, beaten 1 pounds lump crabmeat, picked free of shell 9 buttery crackers 3 tablespoons olive oil	Melt butter in a large, heavy skillet over medium heat. Stir in onion; cook and stir until the onion has softened and turned translucent, about 5 minutes. Stir in the celery, bell pepper, green onion, carrot, and garlic. Continue to cook and stir until vegetables are tender, about 10 minutes more. Season with 1 tablespoon parsley flakes, 2 teaspoons Creole seasoning, basil, pepper, dill weed, oregano, and thyme. Cook and stir until fragrant, 5 minutes more. Transfer cooked vegetables to a large bowl; allow to cool for about 10 minutes. Set skillet aside for later use. Stir beaten eggs into vegetables. Mix in crabmeat and cracker crumbs with your hands, making sure not to break up the chunks of crab too much.

Spicy Cajun Dipping Sauce

1 cup light sour cream
1 tablespoon chili-garlic sauce
2 teaspoons Creole seasoning
2 teaspoons parsley flakes
1 teaspoon paprika

6. Shape crab mixture into twelve small cakes.
7. Heat coconut oil in the skillet over medium high heat.
8. Pan-fry crab cakes in batches until golden brown on each side, about 3 minutes.
9. To make dipping sauce: Whisk together the light sour cream, chili-garlic sauce, 2 teaspoon Creole seasoning, 2 teaspoon parsley flakes, and paprika.

As a father of nine, life can get busy. I look for recipes that are satisfying, tasty, and easy to make—taking a fraction of the time that it took my mother to make us a hearty meal.

This recipe packs all the flavor of a good slow-cooked stovetop jambalaya full of hearty vegetables. It cooks and simmers in that Southern Louisiana flavor without spending time standing over the stove stirring the pot.

Crock Pot Jambalaya

Ingredients:	Directions:
1 pound skinless, boneless chicken breast halves, cut into 1-inch cubes 1 pound andouille sausage, sliced 3 fresh tomatoes diced 1 large sweet onion, diced 1 large green bell pepper, diced 1 cup chopped celery 1 cup low sodium chicken broth 2 teaspoons dried oregano 2 teaspoons dried parsley 3 teaspoons Cajun seasoning 1 teaspoon cayenne pepper 1/2 teaspoon dried thyme 1 pound shrimp without tails	In a crock pot, mix the chicken, sausage, tomatoes, onion, green bell pepper, celery, and broth. Season with oregano, parsley, Cajun seasoning, cayenne pepper, and thyme. 2. Cover and cook 6–7 hours on low, or 2–3 hours on high. Stir in the shrimp during the last 45 minutes of cook time.

Lemon Garlic Shrimp

Ingredients:	Directions:
1 1/2 tablespoons olive oil 1 pound shrimp, peeled and deveined Salt to taste 6 cloves garlic, finely minced 1/4 teaspoon red pepper flakes 2 tablespoons lemon juice 1 1/2 teaspoons red wine vinegar Zest of 1 Lemon 1/3 cup chopped flat-leaf parsley, divided 2 tablespoons coconut oil 1 tablespoon honey	Heat olive oil in a heavy skillet over medium heat until it just begins to smoke. Place shrimp in an even layer on the bottom of the pan and cook for 1 minute without stirring. Season shrimp with salt; cook and stir until shrimp begin to turn pink, about 1 minute. Stir in garlic and red pepper flakes, coconut oil, and honey. Cook and stir 1 minute. Stir in lemon juice, red wine vinegar, and half the parsley. Cook 2–3 minutes. Remove shrimp with a slotted spoon and transfer to a bowl. Continue to cook sauce, adding 2 teaspoons water. Cook about 2 minutes. Season with salt to taste. 6. Serve shrimp topped with the pan sauce. Garnish with lemon zest and remaining flat-leaf parsley.

Sweet and Spicy Slow Cooker Chicken Legs

Ingredients:	Directions:
10 chicken drumsticks 1 (10-ounce) bottle hot sauce 4 tablespoons brown sugar 1/2 teaspoon garlic powder 1/2 teaspoon onion powder Salt and pepper to taste 1 1/2 cups blue cheese salad dressing	Place drumsticks in a slow cooker and sprinkle evenly with brown sugar. Pour hot sauce over chicken. Season with garlic powder, onion powder, salt, and pepper. Cover and cook on high for 2 1/2 hours, or until tender. Serve chicken legs with blue cheese dressing on the side.

Turkey Cabbage Rolls

Ingredients:	Directions:
12 leaves cabbage 1 cup cooked white rice 1 egg, beaten 1/4 cup almond milk 1/4 cup minced onion 1/4 cup minced garlic 1 pound lean ground turkey meat 1 1/4 teaspoons salt 1 1/4 teaspoons ground black pepper 1 (8-ounce) can tomato sauce 2 tablespoons brown sugar 1 tablespoon lemon juice 1 teaspoons Worcestershire sauce	Bring a large pot of water to a boil. Boil cabbage leaves 2 minutes. Drain. In a large bowl, combine 1 cup cooked rice, egg, milk, onion, garlic ground turkey, salt, and pepper. Place about 1/4 cup of meat mixture in center of each cabbage leaf and roll up, tucking in ends. Place rolls in slow cooker. In a small bowl, mix together tomato sauce, brown sugar, lemon juice, and Worcestershire sauce. Pour over cabbage rolls. Cover and cook on low 7–8 hours.

Sweet Baby Collard Greens

Ingredients:	Directions:
1 tablespoon olive oil 1 smoked turkey leg 1 large onion, chopped 2 cloves garlic, minced 1 teaspoons salt 1 teaspoons pepper 3 cups vegetable broth 2 cups water 1 pinch red pepper flakes 1/2 cup apple cider vinegar 1 pound fresh collard greens, cut into 2-inch pieces	Heat oil in a large pot over medium-high heat. Add onion and cook until tender, about 5 minutes. Add garlic and cook until just fragrant. Add collard greens and fry until they start to wilt. Add vegetable broth and turkey leg. Season with salt, pepper, and red pepper flakes. Reduce heat to low, cover, and simmer for 1 hour and 15 minutes, or until greens are tender.

It's Showtime!

Winter, spring, summer, or fall, the urge to grill arises in us all! This recipe is here to satisfy the urge for that backyard grilling while serving up a healthy meal for the whole family!

This Grilled Citrus Chicken recipe is near and dear to my heart. I remember living for that smoky grilled chicken breast that was sure to be on the menu for family gatherings and weekend dinners. The flavor from the grill is like no other. This recipe gives you the same experience; however, I add a citrusy twist. You can use this recipe to create a fabulous citrus chicken breast in about 20 minutes. Save on time and calories but sacrifice nothing on flavor. The burst of flavor from the citrus glaze will leave a party on your palate.

Grilled Citrus Chicken

Ingredients:	Directions:
3 tablespoons low-sodium soy sauce 2 tablespoons honey 1 tablespoon sesame oil 1 teaspoon lime juice 2 teaspoons pineapple juice 1 teaspoon chopped garlic 4 skinless, boneless chicken breast halves	In a shallow container, blend soy sauce, honey, sesame oil, lime juice, pineapple juice, and garlic. Place chicken breast halves into the mixture and turn to coat. Cover and marinate in the refrigerator at least 30 minutes. Preheat an outdoor grill for high heat. Lightly oil the grill grate. Discard marinade and grill chicken 10–12 minutes on each side, until juices run clear.

High Country Boil

Ingredients:	Directions:
3 tablespoons seafood seasoning (Weeziana Girl), or to taste 5 pounds new potatoes 3 (16-ounce) packages cooked kielbasa sausage, cut into 1-inch pieces 8 ears fresh corn, husks and silks removed 5 pounds whole crab, broken into pieces 4 pounds fresh shrimp, peeled and deveined 2 pounds fresh crawfish	Heat a large pot of water over an outdoor cooker (or medium-high heat indoors). Add Weeziana Girl Seasoning to taste and bring to a boil. Add potatoes and sausage and cook for about 15 minutes. Add corn and crab; cook for another 10 minutes, then add the crawfish and shrimp when everything else is almost done. Cook for another 15 minutes. Drain off water and pour contents out onto a picnic table covered with newspaper. Grab a paper plate and a beer and enjoy!

Chipotle Toasted Okra

Ingredients:	Directions:
18 fresh okra pods, sliced in half lengthwise 1 tablespoon olive oil 2 teaspoons kosher salt, or to taste 1 teaspoon ground cinnamon 1 teaspoon chipotle powder	1. Preheat oven to 425 degrees F. 2. Arrange okra slices in one layer on a foil-lined cookie sheet. Drizzle with olive oil and sprinkle with salt, cinnamon, chipotle, and pepper. Bake for 10–15 minutes.

Country Tea Marinated Steak

Ingredients:	Directions:
2 (16-ounce) beef sirloin steaks 1 cup brewed tea 2 tablespoons teriyaki sauce 2 tablespoons turbinado sugar (e.g., Sugar in the Raw) 1/2 teaspoon smoked paprika 1/2 salt 1/2 teaspoon black pepper 1/2 teaspoon garlic powder	Preheat grill for high heat. Place steaks in a large baking dish. In a bowl, mix together tea, teriyaki sauce, and sugar. Pour sauce over steaks, let sit about 15 minutes. Sprinkle with smoked paprika, pepper, and garlic powder; set aside for 10 minutes. Turn steaks over, sprinkle with remaining pepper and garlic powder, and continue marinating for 10 more minutes. Remove steaks from marinade. Pour marinade into a small saucepan, bring to a boil, and cook for several minutes. Lightly oil grill grate. Grill steaks for 7 minutes per side, or to desired doneness. During last few minutes of grilling, baste steaks with boiled marinade to enhance the flavor and insure juiciness.

Dirty South Green Beans

Ingredients:	Directions:
1 pound fresh green beans, washed and drained 7 slices turkey bacon 1/4 cup barbecue sauce 7 shallots, split in halves 1 1/2 teaspoons garlic powder	Preheat oven to 350 degrees F. Place green beans in a 9-inch x 13-inch inch baking pan. Cook turkey bacon in skillet for 4 minutes, until slightly cooked. Dice bacon and lay on top of the green beans. Combine barbecue sauce, garlic powder, and shallots in a small bowl. Pour mixture over the green beans and diced bacon. Bake uncovered for 40 minutes.

Creole Shrimp Stew

Ingredients:	Directions:
1 tablespoon coconut oil 1/2 cup chopped green bell pepper 1/4 cup sliced green onions 1 clove garlic, minced 3 large diced tomatoes 1 (8-ounce) bottle clam juice 1 cup low-sodium vegetable stock 1/4 teaspoon dried thyme 1/4 teaspoon dried basil 1/4 teaspoon red pepper flakes 1 bay leaf 1/2 teaspoon salt 1/2 cup uncooked long-grain white rice 3/4-pound fresh shrimp, peeled and deveined Hot pepper sauce to taste	1. Add coconut oil to a large pot over medium heat. Sauté green bell pepper, onions, and garlic until tender. Stir in diced tomatoes, clam juice, and low-sodium vegetable stock. Season with thyme, basil, red pepper, bay leaf, and salt. Bring to a boil and stir in rice. Reduce heat and cover. Simmer 25 minutes, until rice is tender. 2. Stir in shrimp and cook 10 minutes, or until shrimp are opaque. Remove bay leaf and season with hot sauce.

Food Network - Two-time Cutthroat Kitchen Winner

Did someone say ribs? What's a Southern cookbook without some BBQ ribs? It's not! This recipe is here to seal the deal on "Southern Modified!" Who would have thought that you could modify the flavor of a good barbecue rib?

Get ready for the savory Southern flavor of a BBQ rib, offering the sweet, smoky flavor of a brown-sugar honey-glazed rib but boasting fewer calories. We are getting rid of the sugar and replacing it with agave! Yum! Let's get grilling!

Agave-Glazed Ribs

Ingredients:	Directions:
3 pounds beef or pork ribs 1 cup agave nectar 4 tablespoons ketchup 1 tablespoon cider vinegar 1 tablespoon Worcestershire sauce 1/2 teaspoon salt 1 tablespoon smoked paprika 1/2 teaspoon mustard powder	Place ribs in a large pot and cover with water. Cover and simmer for 1 hour or until meat is tender. Drain and transfer ribs to a shallow dish. In a small saucepan, stir together the agave nectar, ketchup, vinegar, Worcestershire sauce, salt, paprika, and mustard powder. Bring to a low boil and cook for 10 minutes, stirring frequently. Cool slightly and pour over ribs. Marinate in the refrigerator for 1 hour. Prepare grill for cooking with indirect heat. Remove ribs from marinade. Transfer marinade to a small saucepan and boil for several minutes. Lightly oil grate. Cook for about 30 minutes, basting with the cooked marinade frequently, until nicely glazed.

Lemon Pepper Parmesan Baked Fried Chicken

Ingredients:	Directions:
1 clove crushed garlic 1/4 cup coconut oil 1 cup dried bread crumbs 1/3 cup grated parmesan cheese 2 lemons zest 2 tablespoons chopped fresh parsley 1 teaspoon salt 1/8 teaspoon ground black pepper 1 (4-pound) chicken, cut into pieces	Preheat oven to 350 degrees F. In a shallow glass dish or bowl, combine crushed garlic with coconut oil. In another small bowl, mix together bread crumbs, parmesan cheese, parsley, lemon zest, salt, and pepper. Dip chicken pieces into garlic coconut oil, then into crumb mixture to coat. Place coated chicken pieces into a lightly greased 9-inch x 13-inch baking dish. Drizzle with remaining lemon pepper parmesan and bake uncovered for 1 to 1 ½ hours, or until chicken is cooked through and juices run clear.

Frozen Margarita Pie

Ingredients:	Directions:
Crust 1 cup finely crushed Graham crackers 1/4 cup white sugar 1/3 cup margarine, melted **Filling** 1 (14-ounce) can sweetened condensed milk 1/3 cup frozen limeade concentrate, thawed 3 tablespoons tequila 2 tablespoons orange liqueur 2 drops green food coloring, or as needed (optional) 1 cup heavy whipping cream	Preheat oven to 375 degrees F. Mix graham crackers and sugar together in a bowl; stir in margarine until evenly incorporated. Spoon mixture into a 9-inch pie plate; press into bottom and up sides of plate to form a firm, even crust. Bake crust in the preheated oven until edges are lightly browned, about 5 minutes. Cool on a wire rack. Mix sweetened condensed milk, limeade concentrate, tequila, orange liqueur, and green food coloring in a large bowl. Beat cream in a glass or metal bowl until soft peaks form. Lift your beater or whisk straight up: the whipped cream will form soft mounds rather than a sharp peak. Fold whipped cream into sweetened condensed milk mixture. Spoon filling into cooled crust. Cover pie with plastic wrap and freeze until firm, about 4 hours. Let stand for 10 minutes before serving.

Old-Fashioned Banana Pudding

Ingredients:	Directions:
2 cups vanilla wafer crumbs 4 bananas, sliced into 1/4-inch slices 1 1/2 cups white sugar 1/4 cup all-purpose flour 2 cups milk 3 egg yolks 2 teaspoons butter 4 teaspoons vanilla extract 3 egg whites 1/4 cup white sugar	Preheat oven to 350 degrees F. Line the bottom and sides of a 9-inch pie plate with a layer of alternating vanilla wafer crumbs and banana slices. To Make Pudding: In a medium saucepan, combine 1 1/2 cups sugar with flour. Mix well, then stir in half the milk. Beat egg yolks and whisk into sugar mixture. Add remaining milk and butter or margarine. Place mixture over low heat and cook until thickened, stirring frequently. Remove from heat and stir in vanilla extract. Pour half of pudding over vanilla wafer and banana layer while still hot. Make another layer of alternating vanilla wafers and banana slices on top of pudding layer. Pour remaining pudding over second wafer and banana layer. To Make Meringue: In a large glass or metal bowl, beat egg whites until foamy. Gradually add 1/4 cup sugar, continuing to beat until whites are stiff. Spread meringue into pie pan, making sure to completely cover pudding layer. Bake in preheated oven for 15 minutes, just until meringue is browned. Chill before serving

Carrot Cake of Love

Ingredients:	Directions:
4 eggs 1 1/4 cups canola oil 2 cups white sugar 3 teaspoons vanilla extract 2 cups all-purpose flour 2 teaspoons baking soda 2 teaspoons baking powder 1/2 teaspoon salt 2 teaspoons ground cinnamon 2 cups grated carrots 1 cup chopped pecans **For Frosting** 1/2 cup butter, softened 8 ounces cream cheese, softened 4 cups confectioners' sugar 2 teaspoons vanilla extract 1 cup chopped walnuts	Preheat oven to 350 degrees F. Grease and flour a 9-inch x 13-inch pan. In a large bowl, beat together eggs, oil, white sugar, and 2 teaspoons vanilla. Mix in flour, baking soda, baking powder, salt, and cinnamon. Stir in carrots. Fold in pecans. Pour into prepared pan. Bake in the preheated oven for 40–50 minutes, or until a toothpick inserted into the center of the cake comes out clean. Let cool in pan for 10 minutes, then turn out onto a wire rack and cool completely. To Make Frosting: In a medium bowl, combine butter, cream cheese, confectioners' sugar and 2 teaspoons vanilla. Beat until the mixture is smooth and creamy. Stir in chopped walnuts. Frost the cooled cake.

Chocolate Silk Cake

Ingredients:	Directions:
• 3 cups white sugar • 1 3/4 cups all-purpose flour • 1 cup unsweetened cocoa powder • 1 1/2 teaspoons baking powder • 1 1/2 teaspoons baking soda • 1 teaspoon salt • 2 eggs • 1 cup milk • 1/2 cup vegetable oil • 3 teaspoons vanilla extract • 1 cup boiling water • **Frosting** • 3/4 cup butter, softened • 1 (4 ounce) package cream cheese, softened • 1 1/2 (16 ounce) packages confectioners' sugar, or more as needed • 1/4 cup unsweetened cocoa powder and 5 tablespoons brewed coffee	Preheat oven to 350 degrees F. Grease and flour two 9-inch round pans. In a large bowl, stir together the sugar, flour, cocoa, baking powder, baking soda, and salt. Add the eggs, milk, oil and vanilla, mix for 2 minutes on medium speed of mixer. Stir in the boiling water last. Batter will be thin. Pour evenly into the prepared pans. Bake 30 to 35 minutes in the preheated oven, until the cake tests done with a toothpick. Cool in the pans for 10 minutes, then remove to a wire rack to cool completely. For the Frosting: Beat butter and cream cheese together in a bowl with an electric hand mixer until creamy; slowly beat in confectioners' sugar, cocoa powder, coffee, and salt until smooth and spreadable.

Chef on Fire

Chef Jernard and Denise cooking

Chef Jernard and Ricky Bell of BBD & New Edition

Chef Jernard getting ready to film

Chef Jernard on set

Printed in the United States
By Bookmasters